HARRY STYLES

BY JILL SHERMAN

AMICUS LEARNING

Inspire is published by
Amicus Learning, an imprint of Amicus
P.O. Box 227
Mankato, MN 56002
www.amicuspublishing.us

Editor: Ana Brauer
Series Designer: Kathleen Petelinsek
Book Designer and Photo Researcher: Emily Dietz

Library of Congress Cataloging-in-Publication Data
Names: Sherman, Jill, author.
Title: Harry Styles / by Jill Sherman.
Description: Mankato, MN : Amicus Learning, 2025. | Series: Inspire | Includes bibliographical references and index. | Audience: Ages 5–9 | Audience: Grades 2–3 | Summary: "Learn about British pop star Harry Styles and his accomplishments as a musician in this biography packed with photos and fact-filled text suitable for young readers. Includes table of contents, glossary, further resources, and index"— Provided by publisher.
Identifiers: LCCN 2024012083 (print) | LCCN 2024012084 (ebook) | ISBN 9798892001069 (library binding) | ISBN 9798892001649 (paperback) | ISBN 9798892002226 (ebook)
Subjects: LCSH: Styles, Harry, 1994—Juvenile literature. | Singers—England—Biography—Juvenile literature.
Classification: LCC ML3930.S89 S54 2025 (print) | LCC ML3930.S89 (ebook) | DDC 782.42166092 [B]—dc23/eng/20240315
LC record available at https://lccn.loc.gov/2024012083
LC ebook record available at https://lccn.loc.gov/2024012084

Photo Credits: Alamy Stock Photo/Kristin Callahan-Everett Collection, cover, Mark Waugh, 7, WENN, 14; AP Images/Charles Sykes-Invision, 12; Getty Images/Dominic Lipinski - PA Images, 8, Jamie McCarthy, 10–11, Jon Kopaloff, 21, Karwai Tang, 15, Kevin Mazur, 4, 6, Matt Winkelmeyer, 17, Mike Coppola, 18; Shutterstock/Dmytro Volkov, 9

Printed in China

Table of Contents

Harry Styles is known for his colorful and sparkly outfits.

Let's Play!

Harry Styles bounces with energy. On stage, he is all smiles. He is playful and joyful. His fans sing and dance along with him. Styles gives his fans the freedom to be themselves. But who is this British pop star?

Listen Up

Styles grew up in Holmes Chapel, England. As a kid, he listened to music with his family. His dad loved rock music. They listened to Pink Floyd and the Rolling Stones. His mom loved Shania Twain. Styles loved it all.

Styles sings with Shania Twain at a music festival in 2022.

Styles worked at a bakery in Holmes Chapel, England before becoming a singer.

One Direction in 2010. Left to right: Liam Payne, Louis Tomlinson, Zayn Malik, Harry Styles, Niall Horan.

The X Factor

The X Factor is a British music **competition**. In 2010, Styles tried out for the show. He made it to the next round but was voted off shortly after. But it wasn't over yet. The judges put Styles in a group with four other boys. They formed a band called One Direction.

BOY BAND

None of the boys knew each other until meeting on the show. The band placed third in the competition.

The band performed on American talk show *Good Morning America* in 2013.

Boy Band Fame

One Direction was a hit! Styles was a fan favorite. The boys made five albums in five years. They **toured** all over the world. They even performed at the London Olympics in 2012.

In 2017, Styles sang on live TV to promote his new album.

Just Styles

By 2015, the boys needed some time off. One Direction went on a break. Styles wanted to make his own music. But what should it sound like? To figure that out, Styles went to Jamaica. He worked for two months on his music. In 2017, he released his first solo album.

Styles and his co-stars wait behind the scenes of the World War II movie, *Dunkirk* (2017).

Screen Time

Styles is also an actor! In 2017, Styles was in his first movie. He was in the movie *Dunkirk*. He played a British soldier. Styles is even part of the Marvel Cinematic Universe (MCU). He appeared in *The Eternals* (2021) as the brother of Thanos.

LEADING MAN

In 2022, Styles starred in the American movie *Don't Worry Darling* and the British movie *My Policeman.*

Trendy Styles

What to wear? **Boas**! Dresses! Nail polish! Styles loves wearing fun clothes. He doesn't care if clothes are meant for one **gender**. When he's not on stage, Styles still likes to wear colorful suits and sweaters.

Styles uses clothing to make a statement.

Styles believes that everyone can make a difference.

Treat People with Kindness

Styles has a song called "Treat People with Kindness." He uses the **slogan** as a reminder. Small changes can make a big impact. Styles tries to make a difference. Styles encourages people to vote, and he uses his concerts to raise money for charity.

Styles at Home

In 2020, everything stopped. The Covid-19 **pandemic** meant that Styles could not go on tour. At home, he spent more time with friends and family. It inspired his next album, *Harry's House*. Styles feels lucky to get to make music and do what he loves.

Styles won two Grammys for *Harry's House* in 2023.

SUPER STATS

HARRY STYLES

Birthday: February 1, 1994

Hometown: Holmes Chapel, Cheshire, England

AWARDS THROUGH 2024:

Grammys: 3

Kids' Choice Awards: 3

MTV Video Music Awards: 4

Teen Choice Awards: 3

ONE DIRECTION ALBUMS

Up All Night (2011)

Take Me Home (2012)

Midnight Memories (2013)

Four (2014)

Made in the A.M. (2015)

SOLO ALBUMS

Harry Styles (2017)

Fine Line (2019)

Harry's House (2022)

GLOSSARY

boa A scarf made with feathers.

competition A contest or a game.

gender The traits associated with men, women, or other gender identities.

pandemic A widespread illness that affects many parts of the world, like Covid-19.

slogan The words used to promote a cause or product.

tour When someone travels and performs a show.

READ MORE

Anderson, Kirsten. **Who Is Harry Styles?** New York: Penguin Workshop. 2023.

Andrews, Elizabeth. **Harry Styles: Everyone's Favorite Performer.** Minneapolis: Discoveroo. 2024.

Schwartz, Heather E. **Harry Styles: Chart-Topping Musician and Style Icon.** Lerner Publications, 2024.

ON THE WEB

All Music
https://www.allmusic.com/artist/harry-styles-mn0002854537

Official Website of Harry Styles
https://www.hstyles.co.uk/

INDEX

About the Author

Jill Sherman writes books about pop stars, baby animals, and robots. She loves that writing allows her to research and learn about new topics. In addition to writing books, Jill sews her own clothes, creates crossword puzzles, and codes in JavaScript.

She listened to all of Harry Styles' music while writing this book.